**STICKER & SHADE**

# COZY WINTER

## BOLD AND EASY COLORING BOOK

**THIS COLORING BOOK BELONGS TO** _____

# THANK YOU FOR YOUR PURCHASE!

WE'RE SO EXCITED THAT YOU CHOSE COZY WINTER: A BOLD AND EASY COLORING BOOK! WE HOPE YOU ENJOY BRINGING THE MAGIC OF THE WINTER SEASON TO LIFE WITH YOUR CREATIVITY. EACH PAGE IS DESIGNED TO CAPTURE THE WARMTH AND BEAUTY OF WINTER, AND WE CAN'T WAIT TO SEE HOW YOU ADD YOUR PERSONAL TOUCH! YOUR SUPPORT MEANS THE WORLD TO US. IF YOU ENJOY THE BOOK, PLEASE CONSIDER LEAVING A REVIEW OR SHARING YOUR FINISHED PAGES WITH US (@STICKERANDSHADE)—WE'D LOVE TO SEE YOUR CREATIONS!

HAPPY COLORING, AND THANK YOU AGAIN!

# COLORING TIPS

HERE ARE SOME HELPFUL COLORING TIPS FOR SINGLE-SIDED IMAGES PRINTED ON AMAZON PAPER:

## 1. USE COLORED PENCILS
COLORED PENCILS WORK WELL WITH PRINTER PAPER AS THEY DON'T BLEED THROUGH. THEY ALSO ALLOW FOR SHADING AND BLENDING TO ADD DEPTH TO YOUR COLORING.
- TIP: LAYER COLORS GRADUALLY TO ACHIEVE RICHER HUES AND SMOOTHER TRANSITIONS.

## 2. AVOID HEAVY PRESSURE
WHEN USING COLORED PENCILS OR CRAYONS, AVOID PRESSING TOO HARD. LIGHT STROKES WILL PREVENT TEARING THE PAPER OR CREATING HARSH LINES.

## 3. GEL PENS FOR ACCENTS
GEL PENS CAN BE GREAT FOR ADDING BRIGHT ACCENTS OR FINE DETAILS. HOWEVER, THEY MIGHT SLIGHTLY WARP THE PAPER, SO USE THEM SPARINGLY.

## 4. MARKERS WITH CAUTION
ALCOHOL-BASED MARKERS CAN BLEED THROUGH AMAZON PAPER. IF YOU USE MARKERS:
- PLACE A SCRAP PIECE OF PAPER UNDERNEATH TO PROTECT THE NEXT PAGE.
- OPT FOR WATER-BASED MARKERS, WHICH ARE LESS LIKELY TO BLEED.

## 5. BLENDING TECHNIQUES
WITH COLORED PENCILS, YOU CAN USE A BLENDING TOOL (LIKE A BLENDING STUMP OR EVEN A COTTON SWAB) TO SMOOTH OUT THE COLORS FOR A MORE POLISHED LOOK.

## 6. LAYERING LIGHT COLORS FIRST
START WITH LIGHTER COLORS, THEN BUILD UP WITH DARKER ONES FOR BETTER CONTROL AND SMOOTH TRANSITIONS.

THESE TIPS WILL HELP YOU MAKE THE MOST OF COLORING ON AMAZON PAPER!

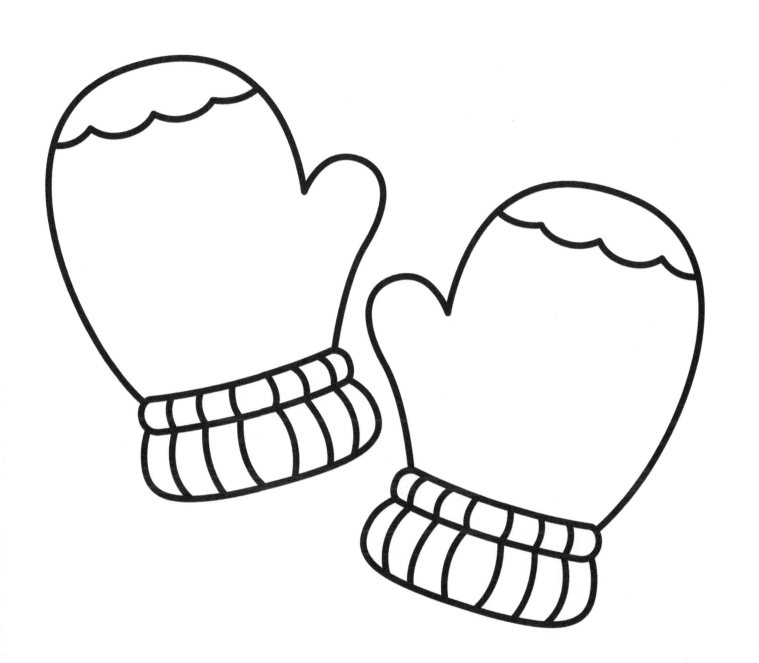

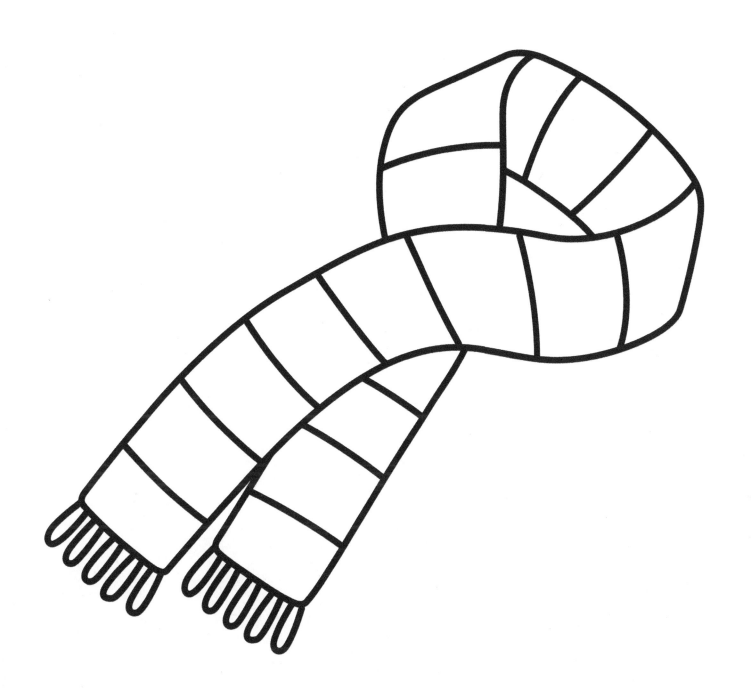

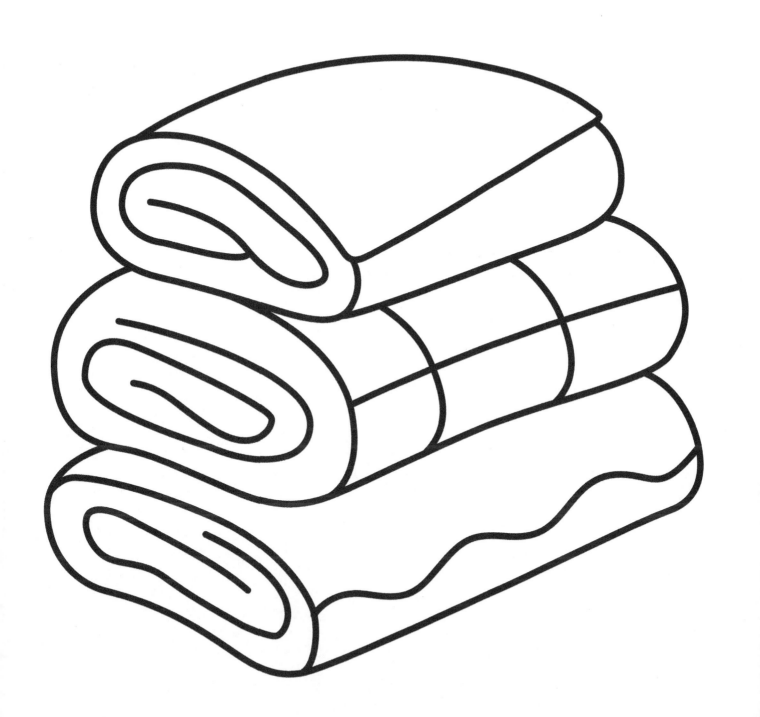

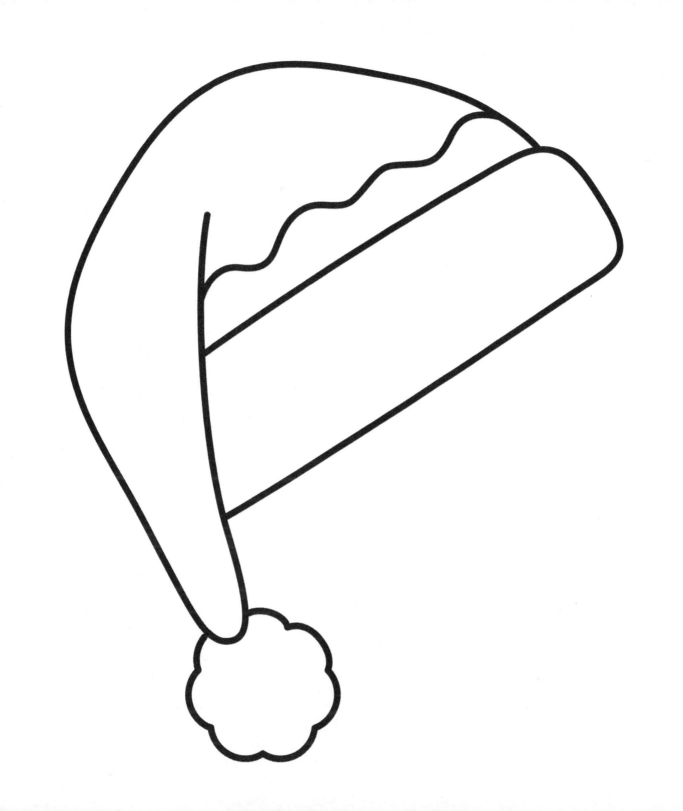

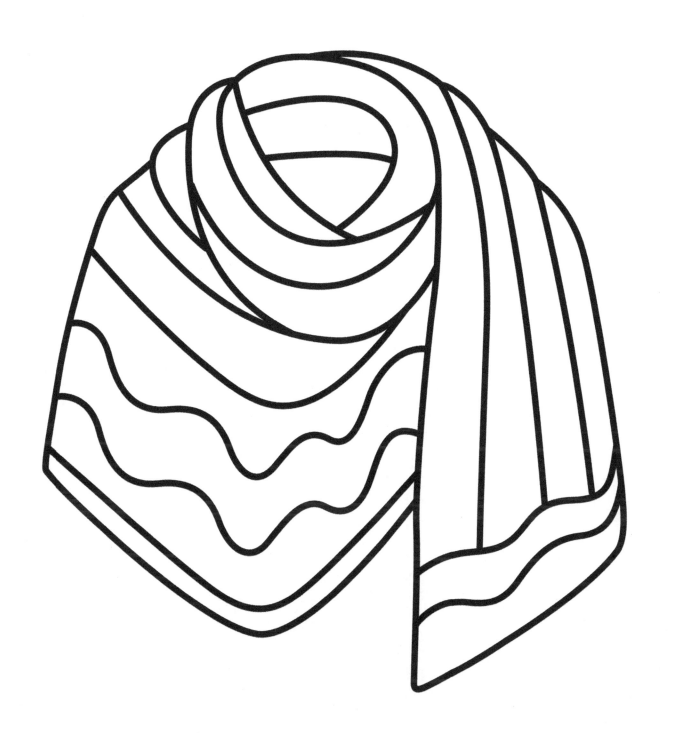

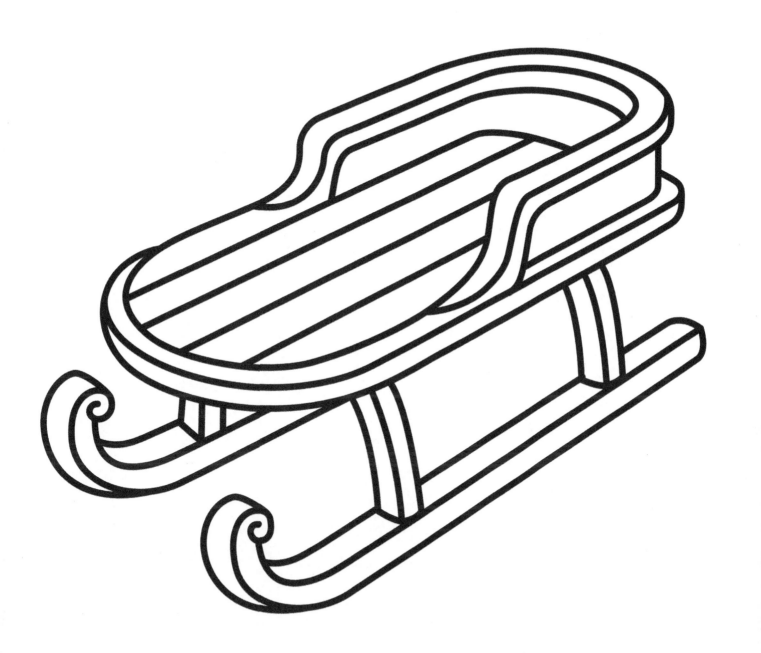

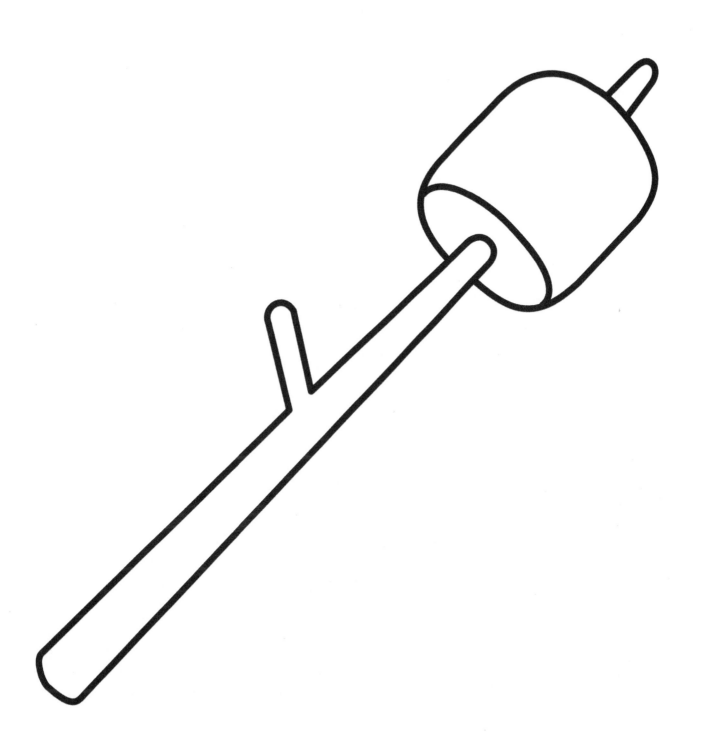